FOOD AROUND THE WORLD

WRITTEN BY GILL BUDGELL

ILLUSTRATED BY TOM HEARD

Designer Terry Sambridge

Author Gill Budgell
Illustrator Tom Heard

Senior Editor Amelia Jones
Senior Art Editor Gilda Pacitti
Managing Editor Katherine Neep
Managing Art Editor Sarah Corcoran
Production Editor Shanker Prasad
DTP Designer Rohit Singh
Production Controller Isabell Schart
Publisher Sarah Forbes
Managing Director, Learning Hilary Fine

First American Edition, 2025
Published in the United States by DK Publishing,
a division of Penguin Random House LLC
1745 Broadway, 20th Floor, New York, NY 10019

A catalog record for this book
is available from the Library of Congress.
ISBN 978-0-5939-6729-4

DK books are available at special discounts when purchased
in bulk for sales promotions, premiums, fund-raising,
or educational use.
For details, contact: DK Publishing Special Markets,
1745 Broadway, 20th Floor, New York, NY 10019
SpecialSales@dk.com

Printed and bound in China

www.dk.com

The publisher would like to thank the following for their
kind permission to reproduce their photographs:

(Key: a-above; b-below/bottom; c-center; f-far; l-left; r-right; t-top)

6 Dreamstime.com: Michelle Minnaar (fcra). **Getty Images:** fcafotodigital (cra);
kabVisio (ca). **8 Getty Images / iStock:** Ocskaymark (bl). **12 Alamy Stock Photo:**
ASP Food (fcr). **Dreamstime.com:** Bignai (cr); Picture Partners (fcra); Steven
Cukrov (fcl); Janet Hastings (bl). **Getty Images / iStock:** kcline (fbl); kuppa_rock
(fcla); SUNGMIN (cl). **Shutterstock.com:** leventina (cra); MaraZe (cla); Paul_Brighton
(br, fbr). **13 Alamy Stock Photo:** Arco / J. Pfeiffer (tc); Facinadora (cla); Alena
Dvorakova (cra); blickwinkel (fcrb); Julian Eales (ca). **Dreamstime.com:** Joseph
Gough (br); Vvoevale (cl); Picstudio (cb); Ronald L (crb); Dmitrii Ulianov (fbl);
Ppy2010ha (fbr). **Getty Images:** Moment / owngarden (tl). **Shutterstock.com:**
Indianstyle (tr); Thao Lan (bl). **20 Shutterstock.com:** guentermanaus (bl).
22 Alamy Stock Photo: imageBROKER / G&M Therin-Weise (cr); Jim West (fcr);
Jake Lyell (bc). **Dreamstime.com:** Kaiskynet (cl). **Getty Images:** Joao Bento da Silva
(fbr). **23 Alamy Stock Photo:** Jake Lyell (cl); Claudia Weinmann (c); Westend61
GmbH (cr); Andrew Mackay (bc). **Getty Images / iStock:** DINphotogallery (bl).
Getty Images: photo by Kris Wong. www.kriswong.com (tc). **24 Shutterstock.com:**
aydngvn (crb); posmguys (clb); Liena10 (cb). **30 Dreamstime.com:** Tien Dung Le
(tr). **Getty Images / iStock:** FG Trade (bl); YinYang (br). **Getty Images:** LUNAMARINA
(tl). **31 Alamy Stock Photo:** a-plus image bank (tr). **Getty Images / iStock:**
IulianUrsachi (br); master1305 (bl). **Getty Images:** Antonio Garcia Recena (tl).
38 Alamy Stock Photo: Hackenberg-Photo-Cologne (bl); The Artchives (tr).
39 Alamy Stock Photo: (bc); GL Archive (tl); Imagedoc (tr). **40 Getty Images:**
Photography by Mangiwau (bc). **41 Alamy Stock Photo:** Pictures From History /
CPA Media Pte Ltd (tl). **Getty Images / iStock:** Anna Rodionova (br). **Shutterstock.
com:** tita s (fbr). **45 Alamy Stock Photo:** Terry Schmitt / UPI (cr). **Getty Images:**
mphillips007 (tl)

CONTENTS

WHAT IS FOOD?

Food and drinks keep us alive. We all need food.

Food consists of proteins, carbohydrates, fats, and other nutrients. Our bodies use nutrients to work well and to grow. And food gives us our energy, too!

For our bodies to grow well, we need food throughout the day, enough food to make us strong, and a balance of different foods to keep us healthy. But not everybody around the world can choose what they eat. Sometimes people have to eat what is available, which depends on what has grown or what is affordable.

Some foods are tasty to us, but not to others. We have different preferences. Some foods are savory, which means they may be spicy or salty. Some foods are sweet, which means they may be sugary.

What is your favorite food?

Rice is a food staple for more than 3.5 billion people around the world.

Around the world, people may eat different kinds of food for their health, their religion, or their personal preference.

People around the world eat food together to celebrate birthdays, festivals, and special times.

LET'S EAT!

People sometimes eat alone and in a hurry, but, around the world, we usually enjoy eating with others and taking our time.

Sheet pan dinners, finger foods, dips, large platters and one-pot meals are ways to prepare food for sharing.

SHARING

Research shows that enjoying food together and sharing is good for our physical health, but also our well-being, too.

WHAT TO USE: UTENSILS

Sometimes people eat with their hands or use bread to scoop food up and into their mouths. Sometimes, people use utensils such as chopsticks or forks, knives, and spoons.

What you use to eat usually depends on where you live, your culture, and also what you are eating.

Using a knife and fork

Using chopsticks

It's tricky to eat peas with a knife, or soup with a fork!

Using hands and bread

EATING RESPECTFULLY

It's important to understand what polite behavior looks like in different cultures around the world, especially when sharing food together. Read on for some examples.

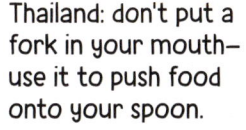

Thailand: don't put a fork in your mouth—use it to push food onto your spoon.

Many cultures around the world, including the Middle East: eat only with your right hand.

North America, Japan, and other cultures: don't talk with food in your mouth.

Remember, it's fun to share food, but always consider how your eating habits may affect other people so that everyone can enjoy their meal!

WHAT TO USE: PLATES AND BOWLS

Plates and bowls can be made from different material.

Natural, such as shells or carved wood: reusable

Human-made from paper: used once and thrown away

Natural, such as gourd halves, leaves, or breads: edible

Human-made from materials such as porcelain, pottery, metal, or plastic: reusable

FOOD AND OUR SENSES

Our senses help us to explore and experience food, but can we use all five of them when we eat, and which senses work together?

Some health conditions, medical treatments, and disabilities can affect the senses and how we experience food. For example, people with sensory processing disorder (SPD) can find certain food textures and flavors too overwhelming to eat.

TASTE

Our tongues taste food. Different parts of our tongues detect salty, sweet, bitter, sour, and umami flavors.

SMELL

Our noses smell food. Taste and smell work together to bring us the flavor of food. If you have a stuffy nose, food may seem tasteless.

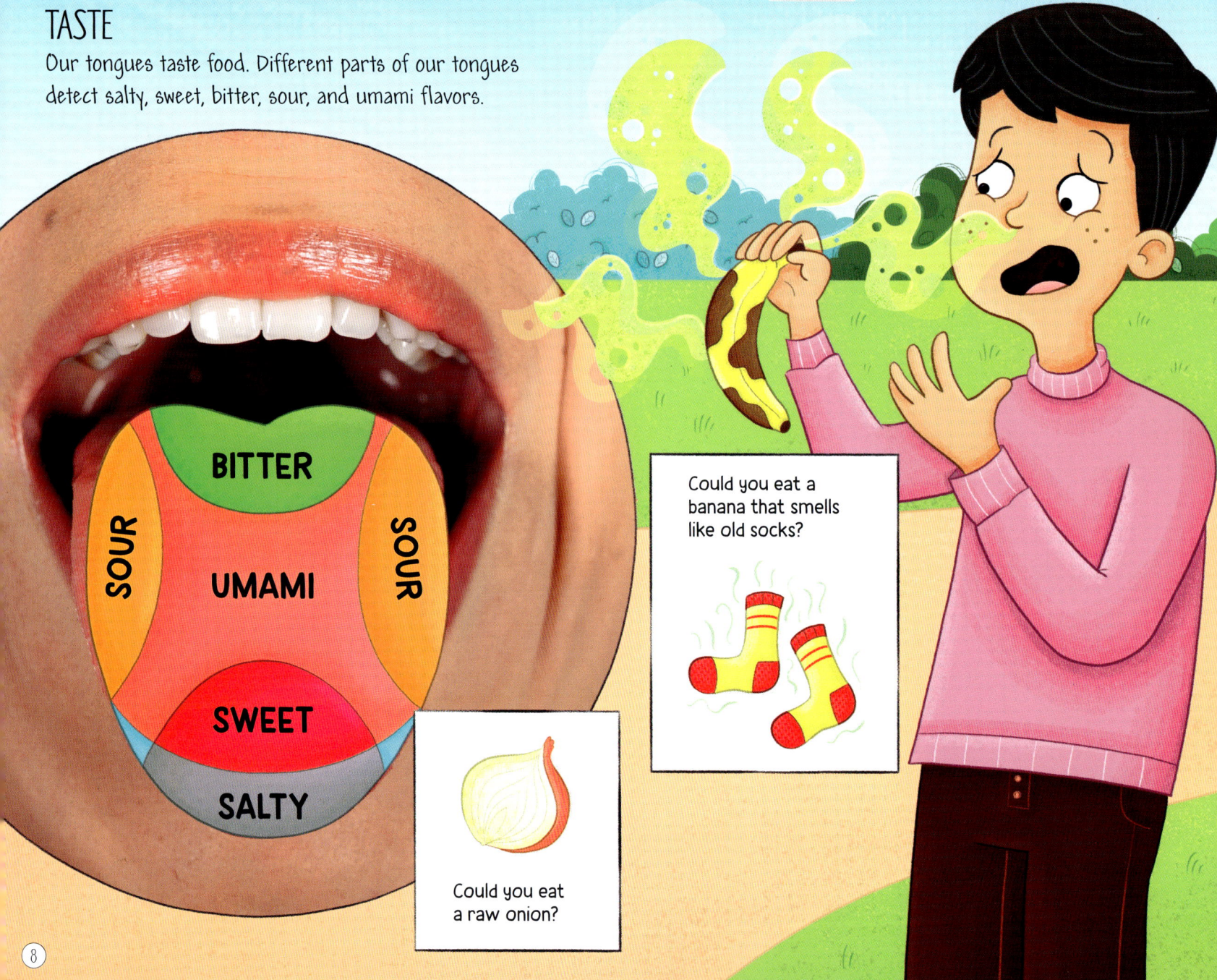

BITTER

SOUR

SOUR

UMAMI

SWEET

SALTY

Could you eat a raw onion?

Could you eat a banana that smells like old socks?

SOUND

Our ears hear the sound of the food we are eating. Sounds such as pop, crunch, and slurp can affect how we feel about what we are eating. If you can't hear your biting sounds, you might think a crunchy apple is less crisp than it really is.

CRUNCH

TOUCH

We touch with our fingers, but we sense textures with our tongues, teeth, and palates, too.

Could you eat something that feels slimy and sticky without looking?

SIGHT

Our eyes see what we are eating and tell our brains what to expect when we taste it. We taste what we think we should, even if it doesn't look right.

Could you eat blue-colored baked beans?

Our senses can play tricks on us, but generally they help us make good decisions about the food we eat.

FOOD GROUPS

There are five main food groups. Eating foods from each group gives us a balanced diet and keeps us healthy. But we need to exercise, too! People's dietary needs can vary based on factors such as their personal choices, culture, and medical needs.

CARBOHYDRATES

These give us energy, calcium, and B vitamins.

Some experts recommend 3–5 servings a day, but people's needs can vary.

FRUITS AND VEGETABLES

Whether fresh, frozen, canned, dried, or juiced, these are packed with vitamins, antioxidants, natural sugars, and fiber to help keep our digestive systems healthy.

Some experts recommend about 5 servings a day.

DAIRY

Foods made from or including milk are called "dairy." Plant-based milks, such as oat milk, are dairy alternatives. Dairy products include milk from animals such as cows or goats. They give us calcium, protein, and vitamins to help keep bones and teeth healthy. Some people are "lactose intolerant," which means an enzyme in dairy can make them sick. They need to choose lactose-free products to meet their needs.

Some experts recommend about 3 servings a day.

PROTEINS

These help to grow and repair the body, just like building blocks. They also provide iron and other vitamins and minerals. There are both animal- and plant-based proteins.

Some experts recommend 2–3 servings a day.

FATS AND SUGARS

These are important sources of energy for our bodies. Sugar can be a quick energy source but should be limited, whereas healthy fats are essential for our diet.

Food groups are the same around the world, but are shown in different ways. On this page, the food groups are shown on a wheel. In China, they are shown in the shape of a pagoda and, in Qatar, inside a clam shell.

AN A-Z OF BREAD

Bread is a staple food, which means that people from all around the world eat it. Most breads are made from a mix of some kind of flour, plus salt, water and sometimes yeast, sugar, milk, or butter. Explore this A-Z of breads and where they are eaten.

A

ANPAN: JAPAN
Sweet buns filled with red bean paste

F

FOCACCIA: ITALY
Flat, oily bread, sometimes like a pizza

G

GRISSINI: ITALY
Crunchy sticks made from semolina flour and, sometimes, honey

L

LAVASH: ARMENIA, AZERBAIJAN, IRAN, TURKEY
A thin flatbread, soft when fresh and crispy when dry

B

BAGEL: POLAND, CANADA, USA
Slightly chewy bread shaped like a ring, boiled and then baked

E

EGG BREAD: KOREA
Sweet, fluffy bread with a whole egg inside

H

HOKKAIDO MILK BREAD: JAPAN
Soft and airy bread with a golden-brown crust, sometimes called shokupan

K

KNÄCKEBRÖD: SWEDEN, DENMARK, NORWAY
Crispy flatbread made from rye and oat or wheat flour

C

CORNBREAD: SOUTHERN USA
Sweet-tasting bread made from corn or maize, also known as mealie bread

D

DAMPER: AUSTRALIA
Thick homemade bread, cooked on an open fire

I

INJERA: ETHIOPIA, ERITREA
Spongy, sour flatbread made from the seeds of a grass called Teff

J

JOHNNYCAKE: SOUTHERN USA, CARIBBEAN
A bread ball with a crisp crust and a soft middle, made from corn batter and fried on a hot griddle

M
MÁNTÓU: CHINA
A soft white steamed bun

T
TORTILLA: MEXICO
A round, thin flatbread made from cornmeal

U
UTTAPAM: SOUTH INDIA
A thick pancake made with fermented lentil rice batter, topped with onions and other vegetables

The oldest bread is over 14,000 years old and was found in the Black Desert in Jordan. It was made from flour and the roots of wild plants, mixed with water to make a dough and cooked on hot stones.

N
NAAN: WEST, CENTRAL AND SOUTH ASIA; MIDDLE EAST
A soft flatbread made with yogurt and olive oil

S
SODA BREAD: IRELAND
Crumbly bread that's quick to make, made with buttermilk and sodium bicarbonate instead of yeast

V
VÁNOČKA: CZECH REPUBLIC, SLOVAKIA
A sweet bread with dried fruit and nuts added

O
OBI NON: AFGHANISTAN, UZBEKISTAN
A flatbread cooked in a clay oven or on a baking stone

R
ROTI: INDIA, CARIBBEAN, SOUTH ASIA, SOUTH AFRICA
A dense, thin flatbread

W
WOTOU: NORTHERN CHINA
A steamed bread made from cornmeal

Z
ZOPF: SWITZERLAND, AUSTRIA, GERMANY
Rich, buttery, and braided bread

P
PUFF PUFF: NIGERIA AND OTHER WEST AFRICAN COUNTRIES
Fried dough, like a doughnut

Q
QISTIBI: THE TATARSTAN AND BASHKORTOSTAN REGIONS OF RUSSIA
A roasted flatbread with a savory filling

X
EXTRA GARLICKY GARLIC BREAD: USA, EUROPE
A white bread, spread with garlic butter and warmed

Y
YUFKA: TURKEY
A very thin flatbread with a sweet or savory filling

DELICIOUS DUMPLINGS

Dumplings are a staple food and enjoyed by people all around the world. But this one small word names foods that look very different for different cultures.

WHAT ARE THEY?

They are small lumps of dough usually wrapped around sweet or savory fillings.

But they may have no filling!

Apple dumplings from the USA are baked until the pastry is golden brown.

They are usually cooked by simmering or steaming.

But they may be baked or fried!

Shish Barak from the Middle East have a spicy, savory filling and are served with a yogurt sauce.

Banku steamed dumplings from Ghana are smooth balls made from cornmeal.

WHAT DO THEY LOOK LIKE?

Dumplings can be many different shapes, but they are usually quite small, so you need a few to make a meal.

CRESCENT-SHAPED

Portuguese rissoles, Japanese gyoza and South American empanadas are all crescent-shaped savory dumplings.

ROUND BALLS

Mongolian buuz, traditionally Jewish knish, and West and Central African fufu are all round ball dumplings. Knish and buuz have savory fillings, whereas fufu tends to be served as a dough ball alongside soup or stew.

"Fufu" means a round "mash" made of foods such as plantains, cassava or yams.

POCKETS AND PURSES

Italian ravioli is a flat, square pasta, and tortellini is scrunched like a small purse.

Indian modaks are teardrop-shaped, while Maltese pastizzi are diamond-shaped.

Japanese gyoza are made from thin pastry that wraps around the filling and is pinched closed with the thumb and index finger to seal it before frying or steaming.

Indian samosas are triangular or pyramid-shaped with a spicy, savory filling.

What sort of dumplings do you eat where you live? Which of these dumplings would you most like to try?

KEEPING BALANCED AND HEALTHY

When we eat from each of the five main food groups and exercise, our diet is balanced and we can stay healthy. But what else matters?

HOW MUCH TO EAT

The energy in food is usually measured in calories. The more we eat, the more energy our bodies can use. Not all foods give us the same energy levels so we must choose carefully.

Too many calories can make your body store fat. Too few calories can make your body weak.

Your age and how active you are will affect how many calories you need.

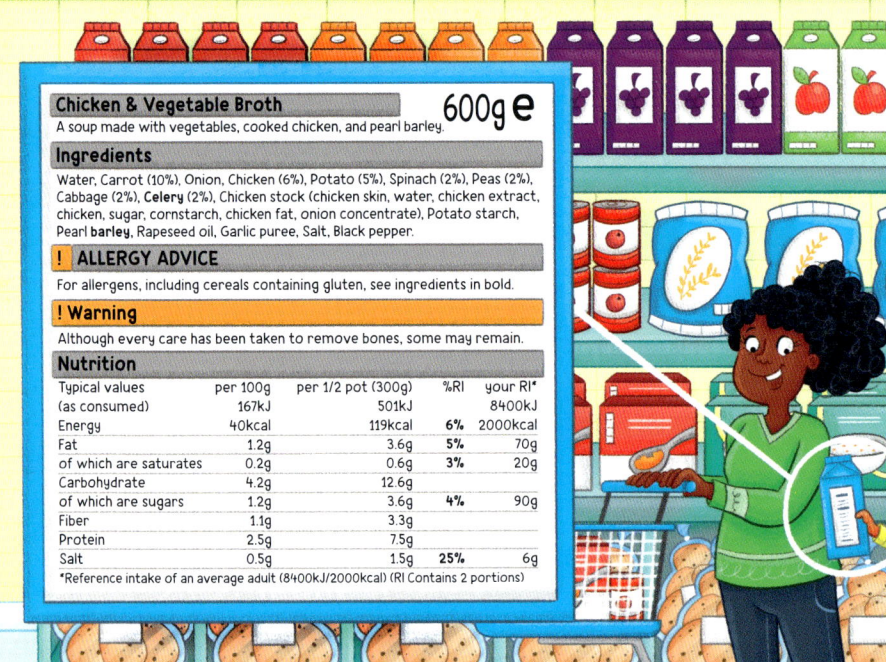

Chicken & Vegetable Broth   600g ℮

A soup made with vegetables, cooked chicken, and pearl barley.

Ingredients

Water, Carrot (10%), Onion, Chicken (6%), Potato (5%), Spinach (2%), Peas (2%), Cabbage (2%), Celery (2%), Chicken stock (chicken skin, water, chicken extract, chicken, sugar, cornstarch, chicken fat, onion concentrate), Potato starch, Pearl barley, Rapeseed oil, Garlic puree, Salt, Black pepper.

! ALLERGY ADVICE

For allergens, including cereals containing gluten, see ingredients in bold.

! Warning

Although every care has been taken to remove bones, some may remain.

Nutrition

Typical values (as consumed)	per 100g	per 1/2 pot (300g)	%RI	your RI*
	167kJ	501kJ		8400kJ
Energy	40kcal	119kcal	6%	2000kcal
Fat	1.2g	3.6g	5%	70g
of which are saturates	0.2g	0.6g	3%	20g
Carbohydrate	4.2g	12.6g		
of which are sugars	1.2g	3.6g	4%	90g
Fiber	1.1g	3.3g		
Protein	2.5g	7.5g		
Salt	0.5g	1.5g	25%	6g

*Reference intake of an average adult (8400kJ/2000kcal) (RI Contains 2 portions)

Check the label on packaged food

Each serving (150g) contains

Energy	Fat	Saturates	Sugars	Salt
1046kJ	3.0g	1.3g	34g	0.9g
250kcal	LOW	LOW	HIGH	MED
13%	4%	7%	38%	15%

In some countries, similar information is provided along with color coding for certain foods.

Red means high levels of a food type, orange means middle, and green means low.

HOW TO MAKE GOOD CHOICES

It is important to understand how to read the Nutrition Facts labels on packaged food so that you can choose foods rich in nutrients.

In some countries, the nutrition facts include information on the calories and recommended serving size of the food, as well as the amounts of:

- sugar
- fiber
- fats
- vitamin D
- sodium and potassium.

KNOWING WHAT WE LIKE OR VALUE

We can choose what we eat based on what we enjoy or value.

- Vegetarians don't eat any meat or fish.
- Pescatarians eat fish, but not meat.

Both often choose these diets for health or other reasons, such as concern for the environment or for animal welfare.

fish

meat

vegetables

milk

eggs

fish

rescue pen

KNOWING OUR BODIES

Sometimes we choose what we eat based on what we know about our bodies.

Allergens are foods that may trigger unpleasant reactions in our bodies such as skin rashes or coughing.

People who know their body reacts strongly to certain foods may carry a rescue pen with them.
The pen helps them to recover quickly if needed.

tree nuts: almonds, pecans

shellfish: crab, shrimp

wheat

soy beans

Good information is important for you.
Make choices that suit you and your body.

EATING THE SEASONS

Some parts of the world have four seasons: spring, summer, fall, and winter. Others have just two: a winter and a summer, or a wet and a dry season.

Growing different foods in different seasons is a natural process and depends on the weather.

HOME GROWN

BUY WHILE STOCKS LAST

FRESH FROM THE FIELD

Food that is in season tastes fresh because it **is** fresh!

It is often cheaper because there is quite a lot available.

It is better for the environment if it's grown locally. There are fewer transportation costs, which means fewer carbon emissions.

WHAT'S IN SEASON?

What's in season also depends on the weather and how well the fruit, vegetables and crops have grown. If it rains too much, root vegetables can rot in the ground. If it's too hot, fruit can spoil on the trees.

· SPRING · · SUMMER · · FALL · · WINTER ·

WHAT'S IN SEASON?

RAINY
When it rains heavily, we feel like eating food to warm us and to help keep coughs and colds away.

DRY
When it's hot and dry, we feel like eating food to cool us. Spices may help to preserve food in hot climates and may have a cooling effect on our bodies.

Not all foods are seasonal. Meat and dairy are available all year.

PARTS OF PLANTS WE EAT

Sometimes we eat parts of a plant and sometimes all of it. We can eat all the parts of plants such as radishes, beetroots and peas. We often eat parts of plants such as fruits, seeds, flowers, stems, bulbs and roots. But not all plants or their parts are safe for us to eat. Always ask an adult if you are not sure.

FRUIT: the sweet and fleshy part of a plant that has seeds

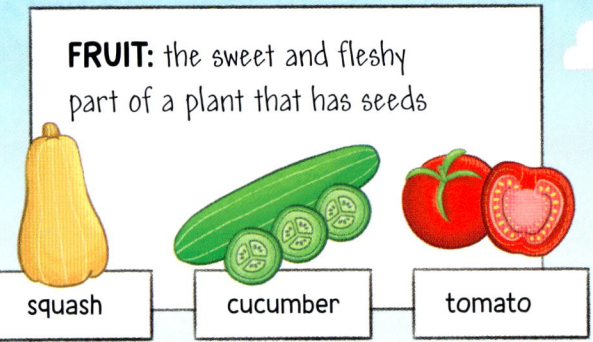

| squash | cucumber | tomato |

CAUTION! ⚠️

The blue sausage shrub grows in the Himalayas. The pulp of its blue fruit is sweet to eat, but the seeds and skin are poisonous.

SEED: the part of a plant that can develop into another such plant

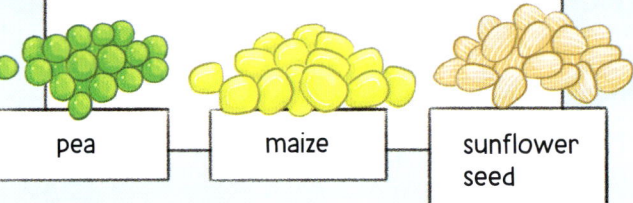

| pea | maize | sunflower seed |

BULB: the part of a plant that is rounded and underground in some plants

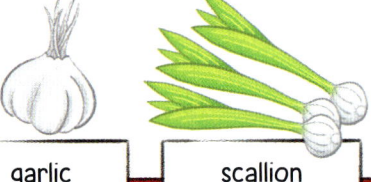

| garlic | scallion | onion |

FLOWER: the part of a plant that is often colored and smells good

cauliflower broccoli artichoke

LEAF: the flat, thin, and usually green part of a plant attached to a stem

lettuce spinach vine leaf

STEM: the main trunk of a plant that can develop buds or shoots

celery leek asparagus

ROOT: the part of a plant that grows down to find water and food in the earth

beetroot carrot ginger potato

FARM TO PLATE

Across the world, farming is essential for food production, although not all food can be grown. So, what is farming?

DIFFERENT KINDS OF FARMING

DAIRY: raising cattle

WATER: raising fish and seafood

ARABLE: producing crops, such as wheat

LIVESTOCK: raising animals, such as sheep or chickens

THE FAIR-TRADE COFFEE JOURNEY

Coffee is grown in over 70 countries across Africa, Central America, South America and Asia. Most coffee is from Brazil, Vietnam, Indonesia, and Colombia.

Fair-trade coffee companies partner with coffee farmers and they work together fairly to create the best coffee.

The farmer plants coffee seeds during the rainy season.

The seedlings are moved to individual pots with special soil and kept in the shade.

When the seedlings are strong enough, they are moved to a shady growing location and planted in rows.

After about four years, the plants may flower.

After a few more weeks, the flowers change to small, green "coffee cherries."

The farmer picks each cherry when it turns red, and removes the green beans from inside.

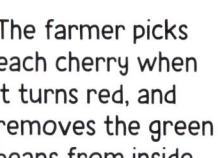

Urban farming grows produce in a town or city.

Intensive farming tries to make as much produce as possible, using human-made chemicals.

Organic farming focuses on producing food without using human-made chemicals that could harm the environment.

Climate, altitude, soil type and landscape all affect how land is used for farming.

The beans are roasted and turn brown.

The fair-trade company pays a fair price for the beans.

The company packages and ships the coffee around the world.

The green beans are dried for a few weeks.

Finally, the coffee is ready to be bought and drunk!

Remember that you too can be a farmer. Try "grow your own" projects at home or school.

FOOD PACKAGING, RECYCLING AND WASTE

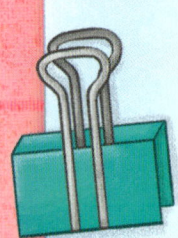

FOOD PACKAGING

Food packaging covers and protects the food we buy.

It can be made of different materials, such as metal, glass, plastic, cardboard, and even wax.

Some packaging materials are compostable, such as bamboo, molded fiber, and sugarcane fiber. These materials break down naturally. Compostable packaging may also be called eco-friendly, sustainable, or green packaging.

Not all food is packaged, but when it is, how do we know if it is eco-friendly?

 RECYCLING

Food packaging usually provides recycling information. Look out for these symbols to guide you:

SYMBOL	♻	BPI COMPOSTABLE	70 GL	41 ALU	1 PETE
CAN IT BE RECYCLED?	Yes.	No, but it is compostable.	Yes: it is made from glass.	Yes: it is made from fully recyclable aluminum.	Yes: it is recyclable plastic.

Arrows set in a circle with a line through the middle usually means something is not recyclable.

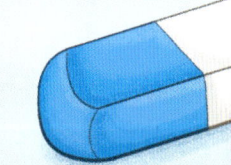

FOOD WASTE

One-third of all food produced in the world goes to waste.

People can reduce food waste by:

✔ buying only what they need

✔ storing food well so that it stays fresher for longer

✔ using food that is left over from one meal to help make another, or freezing it

✔ composting fruit and vegetable waste

✔ if safe, feeding a pet or birds with leftovers

Remember to look out for information on food packaging so that you can make eco-friendly decisions when you buy food. Try to not waste food.

SUPER INGREDIENTS

Ingredients are the different foods we use when making a meal. Super ingredients are foods that are natural, can be used in lots of ways, provide our bodies with essential nutrients and are used around the world.

GARLIC

WHAT IS IT?

Garlic is a plant bulb made up of separate cloves with thin, papery skin that is white, mauve, or purple.

WHY IS IT A SUPER INGREDIENT?

It's rich in nutrients and has medicinal benefits. It adds flavor to a meal.

HOW CAN IT BE USED?

Add to savory dishes:

- uncooked or cooked
- baked whole
- sliced
- chopped
- pressed
- dried.

NUTS AND SEEDS

almond

pecan

pistachio

macadamia

pumpkin

chia

flax

hemp

WHAT ARE THEY?

Nuts are the hard-shelled fruits of plants. Seeds are the small edible plants in seed coats. Most nuts are seeds, but not all seeds are nuts!

WHY ARE THEY A SUPER INGREDIENT?

They're rich in fiber, vegetarian protein, and heart-healthy fats. They add texture to a meal.

HOW CAN THEY BE USED?

Add to savory dishes:

- uncooked or cooked
- whole
- chopped
- flaked
- roasted or toasted
- salted, spiced, or sugared.

BAKER'S YEAST

WHAT IS IT? Yeast is a living single-cell organism that is firm, moist, and creamy colored.

WHY IS IT A SUPER INGREDIENT? It's rich in plant-based protein and nutrients.

HOW CAN IT BE USED?
• Add to make bread rise.
• Use fresh, dried, or blended.

EGGS

WHAT ARE THEY? Eggs are produced by female birds such as chickens or ducks. They are oval or round objects with hard shells.

WHY ARE THEY A SUPER INGREDIENT? They're rich in many nutrients and high-quality protein. They add flavor and thicken dishes.

HOW CAN THEY BE USED?
• Add to sweet and savory dishes to thicken them.
• Eat on their own, usually cooked: boiled, scrambled, fried, or poached.

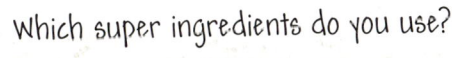

Which super ingredients do you use?

MEASURING AND WEIGHING FOOD

Different countries around the world use different methods and units of measurement and weight, but it's important to be careful and consistent when cooking.

For accurate measuring and weighing we use standard units.

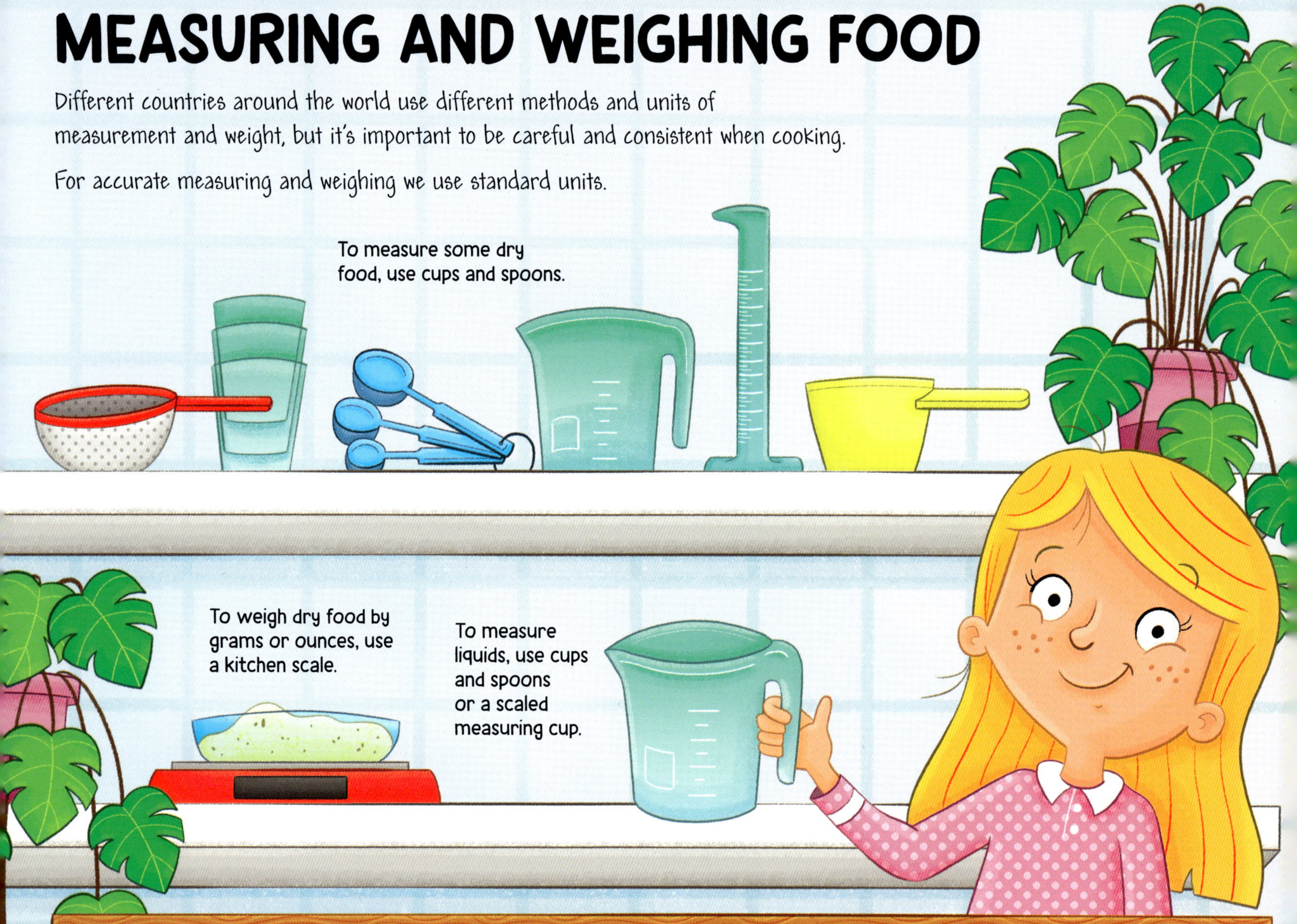

To measure some dry food, use cups and spoons.

To weigh dry food by grams or ounces, use a kitchen scale.

To measure liquids, use cups and spoons or a scaled measuring cup.

For estimated measuring and weighing, use hands for a comparison.

FIST	THUMB	PALM	FINGERTIP	THUMB TIP
		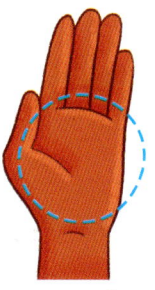		
1 cup	1 ounce of meat or cheese	3 ounces of meat	1 teaspoon	1 tablespoon

BLUEBERRY ROCK CAKES

INGREDIENTS

1 ¾ cup / 200 g almond flour

¾ cup / 75 g blueberries

¼ cup / 60 ml oat milk (or any plant-based milk)

1 tsp baking powder

3 tbsp honey (or maple syrup)

Pinch of salt

2 tbsp melted butter (or coconut oil)

1 large egg (or 1 flax egg for a vegan alternative)

1 tsp vanilla extract

EQUIPMENT

Measuring spoons

Measuring jug

Kitchen scale

Sieve

Large mixing bowl

Wooden spoon

Whisk

Baking paper on a baking tray

METHOD

1. Gather the equipment and prepare the ingredients.

2. Weigh the flour and blueberries on the scale. Measure the milk.

3. Sift the flour into the mixing bowl.

4. Add the baking powder, honey or maple syrup, and salt. Stir to mix.

5. Pour in the melted butter or coconut oil. Stir to mix.

6. Whisk in the egg, vanilla and milk.

7. Add the blueberries. Stir to mix.

8. Drop 2 tbsp of the mixture onto the baking paper for each rock cake. Tip: Pat it flat, but not too thin. Make about six.

9. Bake at 350°F until golden on top.

10. Leave to cool. **Enjoy!**

How could you measure ground ginger? How could you weigh rice?

TASTES OF THE WORLD

Food is part of culture and identity: who you are, where your family comes from, and where you live! Read about these children and the foods they enjoy, but remember the food they love is just a small part of a much broader, rich variety of dishes from each culture.

Arturo

¡Qué rico!

ARTURO is ten years old and lives in Mexico City. He loves the street food scene, especially shrimp tacos.

FUN FACT

MEXICO has the highest number of edible insects. They're enjoyed as a nutritious food source: Dishes can include insect eggs soaked in butter, chocolate-covered locusts, and candy-covered worms.

CAMILA is eight years old and lives in a large city in Salvador, Brazil. She loves to eat sweet cocada on the beach!

Mmm Delicia!

Camila

COCADA

A sweet treat made with coconut, eggs, and condensed milk

FUN FACT

CHOCOLATE comes from the cacao plant, which is native to the Amazon Basin. Indigenous peoples in Central and South America cultivated it for thousands of years before it became the basis of modern-day chocolate.

DARIO is nine years old and lives in San Sebastian in the Basque region of Spain. It is famous for pintxos (snacks). Dario's favorite is rabas, a type of fried squid.

Goxoa!

Dario

RABAS

Battered rings of squid dipped in creamy alioli

FUN FACT

IN BASQUE, pintxo means "spike." Many pintxo snacks are served on skewers.

FUN FACT

IN ETHIOPIA, people enjoy salty popcorn or roasted nuts with their sweet, hot coffee.

t'afach'i

Mazaa

MAZAA is ten years old and lives in Mosebo, a village in Ethiopia. Mazaa's name means "aroma," and she loves the aroma of coffee brewing with sugar or spices.

What would you write about yourself and the food where you live?

NATIONAL DISHES AROUND THE WORLD

For many countries, it is hard to choose just one dish when there are so many to choose from. Here are ten examples of tasty dishes from around the world, but there are many, many more to discover!

NORTH AMERICA

USA: Burgers can be meat- or plant-based. They're served on a bun, with oodles of delicious toppings and sides.

ENGLAND: Roast dinner is roasted meat traditionally served on a Sunday, with a Yorkshire pudding, vegetables, and gravy.

SOUTH AMERICA

JAMAICA: Ackee fruit looks a bit like scrambled egg when cooked, but tastes buttery and nutty. When it's served with salt-cured cod, onions, and tomatoes, you have ackee and saltfish!

PERU: Ceviche is a simple dish of raw fish, citrus juices, and vegetables.

BELGIUM: In moules-frites, fresh mussels are cooked in oil and liquids, with garlic, onions and herbs, and served with potato fries, also called "frites."

LEBANON/SYRIA: Kibbeh is a mix of ground lamb, bulgur wheat, and seasonings. It is best eaten with lots of other appetizers, known as meze.

KOREA: Bulgogi is made of thinly sliced beef marinated in oils, herbs, and spices before grilling. It's served in a lettuce leaf with some kimchi for maximum yumminess.

EUROPE

ASIA

THAILAND: Pad Thai is a stir-fried rice-noodle dish, served with shrimp, peanuts, scrambled egg, and bean sprouts.

AFRICA

AUSTRALIA: Mix a rich onion and mushroom gravy with ground meat and cheese. There you have it: meat pie! Vegetarian versions are available.

AUSTRALIA

TUNISIA: Couscous can be cooked many different ways: steamed, fluffed, and served with vegetables.

Which dish would you most like to try?

STREET FOOD

Street food is about buying and eating food at a market or from a street stall, rather than going into a restaurant or café. It's a relaxed way to enjoy some of the best food around the world. There is something for everyone!

PHILIPPINES

INDIA

TURON
(banana fritters);
BUKO JUICE
(coconut juice)

PANI PURI (crispy balls stuffed with vegetables); **BHAJIS** (vegetable fritters)

SOUTHWEST ASIA, NORTH AFRICA

SPAIN

FUN FACT!
Tagine is a dish named after the pot it is cooked in.

FUN FACT!
Churros were first introduced by Spanish shepherds and possibly named after a breed of sheep called churra.

Many stalls offer food that is authentic to their countries and cultures of origin.

TAGINE
(a spicy hotpot);
FALAFEL
(chickpea fritters)

PAELLA (rice mixed with meat, fish, and vegetables); **CHURROS** (sugary doughnuts)

NIGERIA

INDO-CHINESE

AKARA (deep-fried bean cakes); **KULI KULI** (crispy peanut snacks)

VIETNAM

LOLLIPOP CHICKEN (chicken drumsticks that you eat like a lollipop); **GOBI MANCHURIAN** (deep-fried cauliflower)

TEX-MEX: TEXAS-MEXICO

PHO (noodles); **BANH MI** (filled bread rolls)

FAJITAS (grilled meat and vegetables on corn tortillas); **TACOS** (small, soft wraps with different fillings)

Some stalls offer a mix, or fusion, of food from different countries and cultures to create something new.

What fusion of food types would you invent, if you could?

FOOD FESTIVALS

Most festivals and parties provide food as part of the fun, but some festivals celebrate the food itself!

CELEBRATING THE AVAILABILITY OF FOOD

Some festivals celebrate when food is naturally available and ready to be harvested to eat or store. The harvesting of food such as crops, fruits, and vegetables, is celebrated around the world.

The Cherry Festival, Michigan, USA

The Herring Festival, Denmark

In Denmark, the annual arrival of herring is celebrated. Fishing workers compete to see who can catch the most herring in one hour, and the fish are eaten or pickled for future meals.

The Yam Festival, Ghana and Nigeria

In many remote Arctic communities, Indigenous peoples celebrate successful hunts, not just for survival but also as an important part of their culture and respect for the land and animals.

Inuit hunting celebration

CELEBRATING STORY TRADITIONS

Some festivals celebrate stories about food from long ago. The Giant Omelet Festival in France recounts how Napoleon Bonaparte (a general in the French Army), enjoyed an omelet when he stopped off to rest on a journey. The next day, he returned with his army and demanded a giant omelet to feed them all. Now, each year, about 100 volunteers make a giant omelet. They need a forklift to lift the giant frying pan, and the omelet can feed 2,000 people.

What local festivals do you have to enjoy or celebrate food?

FOOD IN ART

Food has been a common theme in art from ancient times until today. But why?

FOOD ART TO CELEBRATE AND BRING GOOD LUCK

Some cultures use seeds to create transient art to welcome guests and to celebrate during festivals.

An old Indian tradition is to write and paint on a rice grain and to then throw it as a symbol of good luck at weddings or other celebrations. Nowadays, people may have a rice-grain cellphone charm!

Giuseppe Arcimboldo (1526–1593) was an Italian court painter. He painted emperors' faces made up of fruit, vegetables and flowers. People think they represented good times, when food was plentiful.

FOOD ART TO SHOW POPULAR CULTURE

The pop art movement, developed in the 1950s, celebrates popular things of the time. It is art for everyone to enjoy. The North American artist Andy Warhol (1928–1987) created a famous series of pictures of soup cans using repetition and vivid colors. Swedish American sculptor Claes Oldenburg (1929–2022) included cheeseburgers, ice-cream cones, and slices of cake in his art. Yum!

FOOD ART TO SHOW THE EVERYDAY

The Dutch artist Johannes Vermeer (1632–1675) painted everyday foods such as milk and bread.

The French artist Paul Cezanne (1839–1906) painted still life pictures of fruits. These paintings found beauty in the ordinary.

FOOD ART TO SHOW THE JOY OF SHARING

The Swedish artist Karl Olof Larsson (1853–1919) was famous for his paintings of idyllic family life. His own childhood was unhappy, but he found joy in presenting happier times with families and food in his art.

If you were an artist, how would you represent food and why?

39

A TIMELINE OF FOOD

Explore some amazing facts about food through the ages.

PREHISTORY: BEFORE RECORDS BEGAN

Humans living about 2.5 million years ago were hunter-gatherers. They gathered nuts, berries, and insects and hunted animals for meat.

ABOUT 200,000 YEARS AGO

There is evidence from Border Cave in southern Africa that people roasted large land snails because this protein-rich food was filling. They also ate mussels, limpets, and other sea mollusks.

ABOUT 44,000 YEARS AGO

A mural on the wall of a limestone cave on the Indonesian island of Sulawesi shows large mammals being hunted with spears or ropes. This is considered the oldest cave painting of hunting scenes.

FUN FOOD FACT

The global population is thought to have grown from about five million people to around eight billion today. Food is not just for survival, but growth, too.

12,000 YEARS AGO

Agriculture meant people could settle in one place and grow their own reliable supply of food. As agriculture grew, so did cities and civilizations. More food meant more people could survive, and so populations grew, too.

FUN FACT

Cave dwellers might have enjoyed a tasty snack like popcorn. They may have roasted the hard kernels of wild grasses over a fire to make them pop!

REMEMBER!

Long ago, food depended much more on the seasons. Today, new science and farming techniques mean that we can enjoy some foods all year long.

ABOUT 4,700 YEARS AGO: ANCIENT EGYPTIANS

Ancient Egyptians enjoyed all sorts of meat, fish, and fowl (ducks and geese), as well as vegetables. Honey was used in bread and cakes.

FUN FOOD FACT

Ancient Egyptians enjoyed eating figs, dates, and the stalks of papyrus plants.

OVER 2,000 YEARS AGO: ROMANS

Wealthier Romans enjoyed dishes with meats and wheat bread, while Romans with fewer resources often ate meals centred around pulses, such as lentil soup with barley bread.

FUN FOOD FACT

Wealthier Romans might have served roasted dormice, flamingo tongues, or peacocks at feasts for their guests.

ABOUT 1,000 YEARS AGO: THE TANG DYNASTY, CHINA

Experts think that stir-fried noodles were popular. Fruits such as oranges and lychees, and spices such as ginger and cinnamon, were used in cooking, too.

FUN FOOD FACT

A fishy beef jerky called stockfish would have provided nutrients on long sea journeys.

OVER 1,000 YEARS AGO: VIKINGS

The Vikings lived in northern Europe for a very long time before they began exploring and conquering new lands. They raided the treasures they found—and the food.

ABOUT 500 YEARS AGO: THE AZTEC EMPIRE, MESOAMERICA

Maize (corn) was a staple food, along with beans, squash, and avocados. Chocolate was used to make a bitter drink, sometimes with chili peppers.

LAST CENTURY

Processed cheese was first manufactured around 1911 in Switzerland to help people store cheese for longer.

The first fast-food restaurant is thought to have been White Castle, which opened in Kansas, USA, in 1921. They served small, square burgers.

Frozen dinners were introduced in the 1940s. They were served on aluminum trays with three compartments.

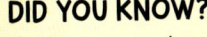

DID YOU KNOW?

The Hadza people of Tanzania are some of the world's last true hunter-gatherers. Some scientists think we should learn about hunting and gathering from these people for our future.

THIS CENTURY

Food is important to everyone, so when people travel around the world, they often take their favorite foods with them. As these foods become popular, they are served in local cafés and restaurants, and everyone can try them.

Instant ramen was introduced in the late 1950s in Japan. Chicken was the first flavor, and all you had to do was add water.

Some of the ways to preserve and cook food have hardly changed at all through the ages:

cooking
salting
pickling
drying
smoking
fermenting

THE FUTURE

Feeding everyone on Earth and taking care of the planet is a major challenge for the future. People are looking for more sustainable ways to eat, including:

- eating more grains, nuts, fruits, and vegetables
- trying insects, jellyfish, cacti, and seaweed
- eating meat grown in a laboratory.

Genetically modified food comes from crops that have been altered to improve certain traits. Sometimes, this can reduce the use of chemicals on the soil.

WHAT DO ANIMALS EAT?

Just like us, animals need food and drinks to stay alive.
And just like us, different animals eat different types of food.

Lions are carnivores.
They will eat any animal
they can prey on.

Giraffes are
herbivores.
Their favorite
food is the
acacia tree.

CARNIVORES

Carnivores are animals that eat other
animals, whether they are mammals, fish,
birds, or insects. They are meat-eating.

HERBIVORES

Herbivores are
animals that eat only
plants. They eat flowers,
fruit, vegetables, grass,
and nuts and seeds.
They are plant-eating.

Venus flytrap

SURPRISING HERBIVORES

Manatees are underwater herbivores. They eat mainly aquatic
plants, but because they are so large, they must eat huge quantities.
This means they regularly grow new molars to replace old worn-out teeth.

SURPRISING CARNIVORES

The Venus flytrap is a carnivorous
plant. It has special spiked lobes
with trigger hairs that snap shut
when triggered by an insect.

Manatee

OMNIVORES

Omnivores eat plants, animals, algae, and fungi, which means that they have more options when one type of food is not available.

DID YOU KNOW?
Humans are omnivores, but that doesn't mean that we have to eat meat. People make individual choices about what they eat.

Raccoons are omnivores. They eat most things!

SURPRISING OMNIVORES

Bees are omnivores. They mainly eat plants, but they also need microbial meat, which is found in pollen and is the protein of bacteria and fungi.

Bees

Choose a favorite animal, and find out what type of food it likes to eat.

FUN FOOD WORDS AND FOOD RECORD BREAKERS

Read these fun food words, tongue twisters and rhymes.

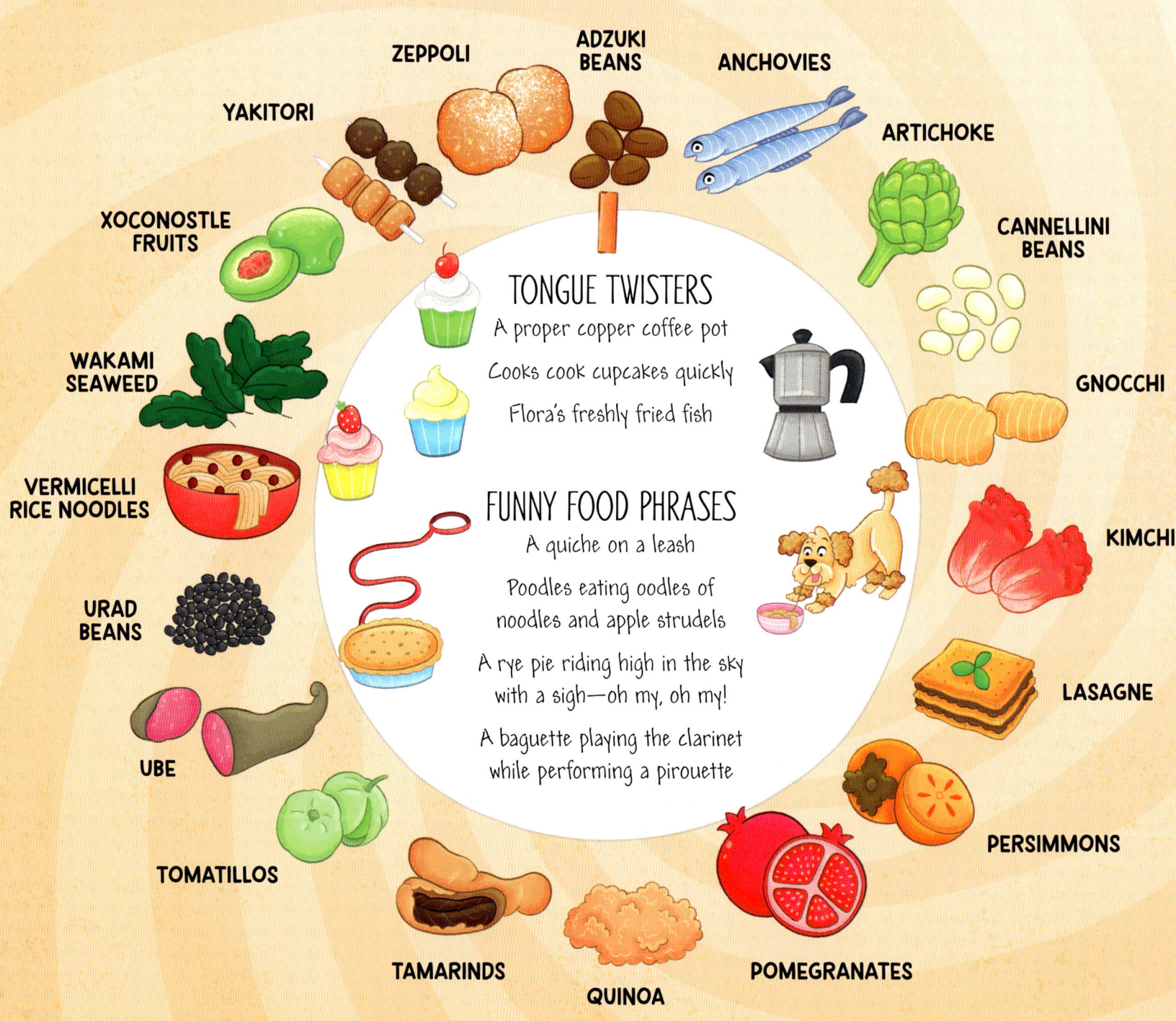

ZEPPOLI

ADZUKI BEANS

ANCHOVIES

YAKITORI

ARTICHOKE

XOCONOSTLE FRUITS

CANNELLINI BEANS

WAKAMI SEAWEED

GNOCCHI

VERMICELLI RICE NOODLES

KIMCHI

URAD BEANS

LASAGNE

UBE

PERSIMMONS

TOMATILLOS

TAMARINDS

QUINOA

POMEGRANATES

TONGUE TWISTERS

A proper copper coffee pot

Cooks cook cupcakes quickly

Flora's freshly fried fish

FUNNY FOOD PHRASES

A quiche on a leash

Poodles eating oodles of noodles and apple strudels

A rye pie riding high in the sky with a sigh—oh my, oh my!

A baguette playing the clarinet while performing a pirouette

Read these amazing facts about food.

3,010 LB (1,365 KG)

This was the weight of the largest scoop of ice cream, which was strawberry flavored made in Wisconsin, USA. That's about 733 containers of ice cream!

100 🇺🇸 PIZZERIAS

That's the most fast-food restaurants visited by one person in 24 hours. The record was set in New York, USA.

1,535 LB (696 KG)

That's the weight of the heaviest pumpkin, grown by Ron Root in California, USA.

🇮🇹 🇭🇷

$7,000 PER LB

That's the world's most expensive fungus: the edible white truffle. It grows underground in parts of Italy and Croatia, and trained dogs dig it out.

🇨🇳 10,119 FT (3,084.32 M)

That's the longest noodle, made in Henan, China.

WORKING WITH FOOD

There are many ways to work with food. For some jobs, such as being a dietitian, you must have a scientific understanding of food to do the job. For others, such as food journalism, understanding food can be helpful but may not be required. For some jobs, for example, being an international development worker, you might choose to learn more about food distribution or pick it up as part of the job.

FOOD EDUCATOR

Studies food in order to teach students about it

DIETITIAN

Assesses, diagnoses, and helps treat people who have dietary or nutritional issues

FOOD SCIENTIST

Develops food and drink products, making sure they are safe for people to enjoy

CHEF

Prepares, cooks, and presents food in hotels, bars, and restaurants

CATERING MANAGER

Runs the food service of restaurants, bars, schools, colleges, and outside suppliers

WAITER OR SERVER

Welcomes guests, explains a menu, takes orders, and brings food to the table

LINE COOK

Keeps the kitchen clean and helps to prepare equipment and food for the chef(s)

FOOD DELIVERY DRIVER

Delivers food in the food industry or to customers, ensuring food safety and quality

FARMER

Grows crops and/or raises farm animals for food production

FOOD PROCESSING WORKER

Produces and packages food, ensuring food safety and quality

FOOD JOURNALIST

Researches, investigates, and presents news for television, radio, and online, ideally with a scientific understanding of food

INTERNATIONAL DEVELOPMENT WORKER

Supports communities in need, often ensuring that people have food to eat and clean water to drink in an emergency

INDEX

GLOSSARY

PAGES	WORD	MEANING
pp4–5	nutrients	things that plants and animals need to live and grow
	food staple	a basic food
pp6–7	edible	able to be eaten
pp8–9	umami	a savory taste, but not sour, salty, or bitter
	palates	the top part of the inside of people's mouths
pp10–11	calcium	a mineral that is important for strong bones and teeth
	vitamins	a group of substances from plants or animals that are important for staying healthy
	antioxidants	things that slow down decay
	minerals	a group of substances from the ground that are important for staying healthy
pp13–14	sodium bicarbonate	a white powder that is used in baking to make bread or cakes rise
	fermented	having yeast or bacteria added to make a chemical change, to flavor it, and so it lasts for longer without decaying
pp16–17	sodium	a mineral in salt
	potassium	a mineral that is important for staying healthy
pp18–19	carbon emissions	quantities of a gas (carbon dioxide) being released into the air
	hydrate	to wet or water something
pp22–23	human-made chemicals	chemicals made by people and often in things like paint, building materials, and nail polish
	altitude	height above sea level

PAGES	WORD	MEANING
	fair trade	trade that is in accordance with an agreement between farmers and companies that aims to make wages and working conditions fair and to make ways of farming longer lasting (often including money to support local community projects)
pp24–25	compostable	able to decay over time and become part of soil
pp28–29	cooking	preparing food by mixing and heating it
	standard units	fixed values to measure things like length or weight
pp32–33	marinated	soaked
	kimchi	a spicy pickled cabbage dish from Korea
pp38–39	transient	short-lived or short-term
	court painter	an artist who paints for a royal family
	still life	art of natural or human-made everyday things
pp40–41	agriculture	farming, including growing crops and raising animals
	salting	keeping food in salt so it lasts for longer without decaying
	pickling	keeping food in vinegar to flavor it and so it lasts for longer without decaying
	drying	keeping food free of water so it lasts for longer without decaying
	smoking	cooking food in the smoke from a slow, gentle fire to flavor it and so it lasts for longer without decaying
	genetically modified	changed scientifically in a way that affects growth and development